How to Write a Report

HOW TO WRITE

A REPORT

by Sue R. Brandt

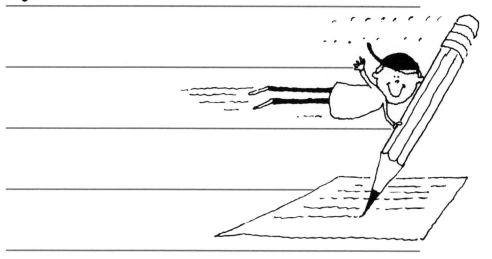

ILLUSTRATED BY
ANNE CANEVARI GREEN

A FIRST BOOK
REVISED EDITION

FRANKLIN WATTS I 1986
NEW YORK I LONDON I TORONTO I SYDNEY

Library of Congress Cataloging in Publication Data

Brandt, Sue R.
How to write a report.

(A First book)
Includes index.
Summary: Step-by-step instructions for writing a
report, including choosing and understanding the subject,
building a bibliography, taking notes, outlining, and
writing the final draft.
1. Report writing—Juvenile literature. [1. Report
writing] I. Green, Anne Canevari, ill. II. Title.
LB1047.3.B73 1986   808'.02   86-9056
ISBN 0-531-10216-5

J
808
BRA

3|87

For
Nan, of University City, Missouri
Howard, of North Hollywood, California
Joel, of Canon City, Colorado
Ricky and Jimmy, of Vandalia, Missouri

Contents

Chapter 1
Who Writes Reports?
11

Chapter 2
What Is a Report?
14

Chapter 3
How to Begin
16

Chapter 4
Your Subject, or Topic
18

Chapter 5
Researching (Collecting
Facts or Information)
30

Chapter 6
Taking Notes
52

Chapter 7
Giving Credit to Others
55

Chapter 8
Making an Outline
57

Chapter 9
Writing Your Report
66

Chapter 10
Book Reviews and Reports
78

Basic Tools for Young
Researchers—A Quick Review
87

Index
91

How to Write a Report

1

Who Writes Reports?

"Reports! Reports!" exclaimed Sandy. "Almost everyone I know is working on reports. My mother came home from her office with a big stack of reports. My brother is writing a report for a hobby magazine, telling how he made his new robot. My father is working on a report for a TV special. It tells how firefighters kept a forest fire from burning up people's houses. I've begun my report about sponges—"

"I know," Tracy said. "My aunt works for a big company. She used to be called the company librarian. Now she's called an information specialist, and the company library is called the information center. Reports flood into her office all day long. She says the people in her company could not do their work without all those reports."

It is true. The work of the world could not be carried out without the many kinds of information contained in reports. Young people write reports for their schoolwork. Astronauts and pilots, teachers, doctors, and medical researchers write reports. Engineers and technologists, designers and inventors, salespeople and advertising experts, police officers and firefighters write reports. Governors and mayors, judges and lawyers—and

almost everyone else who is doing important work—write reports. They also read and study reports written by other people.

And reports are becoming more and more important to more and more people every day. Why is this so? It is because of a great explosion in our times—a knowledge explosion, or information explosion. We live in an Information Age, made possible by the wonders of electronics. And we have an exciting new industry—the information industry.

When you learn how to write reports, you discover what the Information Age is all about. You learn how to research—how to dig for information—and how to get facts together and pass them along to other people. You discover that there are more ways to find information and more places to look for it than you ever dreamed of. Sometimes your search takes you beyond the classroom. You find that people are interested in what you are doing and are eager to help you.

One discovery leads to another. Before long, you begin to feel self-confident and independent. You become a part of the information industry. You join the huge network of people who share the give-and-take of the Information Age.

2

What Is a Report?

In school you do different kinds of writing. You write stories about real or imagined happenings. You write descriptions of what you have seen, heard, read about, or dreamed. Perhaps you write poems, too, and you write friendly letters and notes. Everyone likes to get letters, and almost everyone enjoys stories, descriptions, and poems. Your main purpose in these kinds of writing is to entertain your readers—to give them pleasure.

You also do writing for other purposes. You learn to write a business letter, ordering a name tag for your dog or asking for an autograph on a baseball card. And you learn to do the kind of writing that gives facts, or information, about a certain subject, such as robots, sponges, or how to make the best chocolate-chip cookies. This kind of writing is called a report. The word *report* comes from an old word that means "to carry back." There are various kinds of reports, but most reports are alike in certain ways:

1. Reports are meant to be used. They carry information from writers who have certain facts to readers who want those facts.

2. Reports are meant to give facts. For this reason, writers of reports do not mix facts with their own ideas or opinions. If they

wish sometimes to give their own ideas, they keep those ideas separate from the facts. (In reporting on, or reviewing, books that you have read, you give your opinions freely. Your readers want to know what you think. But that is a different kind of reporting. You will find suggestions about that in the last chapter of this book.)

3. A report can be called a good report if it gives facts *correctly*, as *briefly* as possible, and very, very *clearly*. If it does all this, readers will be satisfied. If it is also interesting, they may smile and nod their approval—or even clap and cheer!

3

How to Begin

The way to learn how to write reports is, of course, to write reports, just as the way to learn how to play soccer, program a computer, or play the drums is to do these things. But you would not expect to be able to do them suddenly, as if by magic. You know that you have to begin at the beginning.

To learn how to do almost anything, you must have a plan, and you must follow that plan, step by step. Here is a plan that most people use in preparing a report:

1. Choose a subject, or use the subject assigned to you.
2. Do some reading or inquiring about the subject so that you can begin to decide what is most important, as well as most interesting to you, and what your readers should learn.
3. Do your research—that is, find the facts that you will need to tell what you think is most important and most interesting about the subject.
4. Make notes of the facts, so that you will not forget anything that is important.
5. Make notes about where you found the facts, so that you can give credit to others.
6. Organize the facts in an outline.
7. Write the first draft of the report.
8. Correct and improve the first draft.
9. Make a neat final copy of the report.

4

Your Subject, or Topic

Subject, or topic, means "what the report is about." Sometimes everyone in the class will have the same subject. At other times you may be free to choose what you will write about.

Suppose, for example, that the members of a science class have an argument about what sponges are. Someone says sponges are plants. Others say they are animals. Still others say that sponges are not living things—that they are made in factories, from chemicals or other substances.

The teacher suggests that everyone find the answer to this question and write a short report about sponges. Because the members of the class are just beginning to write reports, the teacher helps them think about the subject and how they will handle it in their reports:

"First, you need to do some reading or inquiring to learn what sponges really are. As you do this, you will find other information about sponges. Some of it will seem important and interesting to you. Some may seem dull or boring. Anyway, you will discover that you cannot tell everything about sponges in a short report.

"The reports should have three or four paragraphs. If you have three paragraphs, you will have three main ideas. You already know what one of the main ideas will be. It will be the answer to our question, 'What are sponges?' You might write that down now.

"Think about what else seems most important and most interesting for a short report. That is, think about what your other main ideas might be. You may find, for instance, that there are various kinds of sponges. The kinds of sponges, then, might be a main idea. You may discover something about where sponges are found, about how we get them, about the history of sponges, and so on.

"Write down main ideas that you think you want to write about. And see me, if you wish, before you continue your research for facts about sponges."

Here is Angie's report:

Science   Angie Loh
                    Sponges

    Sponges are animals that live in seas and other bodies of water, but they are very strange animals. People once thought they were plants. They have no head or mouth or feet. But scientists now agree that they are animals because of the way they get their food. The New Book of Knowledge says sponges are "a kind of living sieve." They strain food from water that flows into their bodies through tiny pores, or holes.
    There are thousands of kinds of natural sponges, but scientists classify them into three groups by their skeletons. One kind has a skeleton of chalk or lime. Another kind has a glassy skeleton. The kind we use has a skeleton made up of fibers called spongin.

Sponges of this kind are known as common sponges, or bath sponges. When they are alive, they are very dark in color, but they become much lighter when they are dried for use. Some of the other kinds have bright colors and shapes like vases or tree branches or bowls. We also use sponges that are not natural sponges but are made of rubber or other substances.

The natural sponges that we use come from parts of the Mediterranean and Caribbean seas. One place where we get them is Tarpon Springs, Florida. In shallow water, people go out in boats and use long poles with hooks to get the sponges. In deeper waters, divers gather sponges and bring them up in baskets.

Toni's report, like Angie's, told what sponges are and about the various kinds. But Toni's report ended with this paragraph:

I could not believe it when I saw pictures of different kinds of sponges. The shapes and colors were fantastic. Some looked like purple trumpets or huge olives flecked with gold or fuzzy lavender caps with pointed tops. Another one seemed to be a mass of orange-colored tubes standing upright. So I went to the museum to see whether I could find sponges there. I did find some. You should go see them, especially the one called Venus's flower-basket.

Most of the reports were good reports. They answered the main question and gave other important information about sponges. The facts were stated correctly and clearly. Yet each report was special because it showed the writer's own point of view (way of thinking about the subject). When all the members of your class are writing about the same subject, you can make your report special in the same way.

CHOOSING A SUBJECT

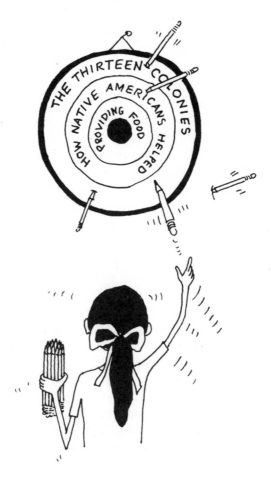

Probably you will write quite a few reports in connection with big subjects that you are studying. Examples of big, broad subjects are the American colonies (the thirteen colonies that became the United States), your own state, a country of the world, the solar system, the world of animals, volcanoes and earthquakes, and electricity and electronics. These big subjects have many smaller parts, and you may study different parts in different grades in school.

When you are free to choose, how do you select a small part of a big subject for a report? You do it by narrowing the subject. Learning how to narrow a subject and pick out a small part, or topic, is important in writing a report. Let us see what "narrowing a subject" means and how you can learn to do it.

In studying the thirteen colonies, you learn something about the many main parts of the subject. The main parts include (1) why people decided to go to the New World, (2) how each of the colonies began, (3) how the earliest colonists provided food, clothing, and shelter for themselves and their families, (4) how the colonies were governed, (5) what schools in colonial days were like, (6) what industries became important in the different colonies, (7) who the leaders of the colonies were and why we remember them.

You discover that each of the main parts is a big subject— much too big for a report. You think, then, about the many smaller parts that might make a good topic for a report. For example, you might think of the voyage of the *Mayflower*, the ways in which the native Americans helped the Pilgrims, the "Lost Colony" of Roanoke Island, how the colonists made candles, why forests were important to the colonists, or Peter Stuyvesant. Which one will you choose? You choose a topic that interests you and that you want to know more about. Choosing a topic that really interests you is important because you do your best work—and you enjoy doing it—when you are enthusiastic about what you do.

The world of animals is truly a huge subject. When you are beginning to write reports, you might choose a single animal or kind of animal that is your favorite or that you are curious about. It might be bears, platypuses, butterflies, eagles, dinosaurs, or any one of thousands of other creatures. Even then, you might discover that the subject is too big for a report. You could narrow it further and choose, for example, one kind of dinosaur or butterfly. When you investigate your chosen topic, you might have some surprises, too, as one member of a class did when she chose her favorite kind of bear—the kind she called the "koala bear." When she learned what koalas really are, she was amazed—but more interested than ever. And her report was the best one she had written. She was excited, too, because she had discovered a big group of animals new to her, the marsupials.

In your study of animals, you discover that marsupials belong to a larger group that scientists call mammals. And mammals, in turn, are part of a bigger class known as vertebrates (animals with backbones). Knowing how scientists divide up the animal world can help you narrow this huge subject and choose a topic for a report. For example, you might be curious about the main differences between two kinds of vertebrates, such as the reptiles and the amphibians, and decide to write a report on that topic. If you are interested in insects, you soon discover how big this subject is. Insects (which belong to the bigger main class called invertebrates—animals without backbones) are the largest single group of animals in the world. There are many different orders (kinds) of insects, and each order is divided into numerous suborders. For a report, you might decide to narrow the main subject (insects) to one of the orders, such as the beetles, and then to narrow the subject of beetles to one kind, such as the ladybird beetle (or ladybug).

Sometimes you pick up bits of information that can give you ideas for reports. For example, you may be fascinated by facts about the size of animals (about which ones are the largest) and about how fast different animals can move, how high they can jump, how strong they are. How about a report with the title "Animal Champions"? Or maybe you have learned that all creepy, crawly creatures are not insects. Neither are all of them bugs, as some people call them. You might plan a report about how spiders, scorpions, and ticks (all classified as arachnids) are different from insects. Or you might tell how the insects known as true bugs differ from beetles.

You discover, too, that parts of one big subject keep coming up in other subjects. In other words, you discover relationships (the ways in which one subject is related to, or connected with, other subjects). Discovering relationships is the best way of learning. And it can give you interesting ideas for reports.

In health class, for example, you may have learned about insects that carry diseases and thus are harmful to people. You probably have learned, too, that many insects are helpful to people. When you think of insects in this way, you discover another way to narrow the subject. For a report, you might write about ways in which insects help (or harm) people, or you could limit the subject even more, to one helpful (or harmful) insect.

In your study of different countries, you learn about animal life new to you. And when you study your state, you may discover that your state has adopted a state animal (mammal), fish, and insect, along with the usual emblems of bird, flower, and tree. An animal new to you, along with information about why it thrives in a certain country, might make a good subject for a report. So would one of your state emblems, especially if you tell why and how it was chosen. When you study conservation and environmental protection, you may become interested in extinct animals (animals that have disappeared) or animals of today that are in danger of disappearing. Within these related subjects, you are sure to find good topics for a report.

Here is a report. Can you tell how Kevin narrowed his subject and how he brought parts of two big subjects together?

Kevin Daly
Bears of North America
Three kinds of bears live in North America. They are American black bears, big brown bears, and polar bears. Big brown bears are of two kinds, the Alaskan brown bear and the grizzly.
Black bears live in most of the wooded parts of Canada, the United States and northern Mexico. Alaskan brown bears live in southern Alaska. Once grizzlies

could be found in all the western parts of North America, but now most of them are in Canada and Alaska. South of Canada they have been driven from all the states of the United States, except parts of Montana, Wyoming, and Idaho. Polar bears roam ice packs and the coasts of the Arctic Ocean

Polar bears were once in danger of disappearing, and grizzly bears still are, south of Canada. Polar bears became in danger when sports hunters began to use small planes and snowmobiles to hunt them. But all the countries bordering on the Artic passed strict laws to protect polar bears. Protecting grizzlies where they now live, in and around national parks, is a different kind of problem. Grizzlies always have needed lots of room, away from people. But people also use the parks. Wildlife experts are trying to find ways to protect the grizzlies and the people, too. That is a hard job.

For another example of how to choose a topic, let us think about the big subject of electronics and the many kinds of electronic devices and machines, such as computers, communications satellites, spacecraft, and robots. All these machines are fascinating because they are changing the way we live, entertain ourselves, get information, treat diseases, and carry on our work. And most of them are big and complicated subjects, as you would discover if you decided to write a report about one of them—robots and robotics (the science of building robots), for example.

The subject of robots can be divided in a number of ways. First, there are two main kinds—true robots and robotlike devices. Then, we can think of robots in two separate worlds—the real world and the world of fantasy and science fiction. And robotlike devices have a long history.

Narrowing the subject of robots can be fun. If you are especially interested in the world of fantasy, you might write about famous robotlike characters in stories or the movies, or you might choose the three "Laws of Robotics" created by the writer Isaac Asimov. If robots of the real world appeal to you, you might want to report on industrial robots and the kinds of work they do in factories, about how robots are "taught" to do work, about "show robots," or about some robotlike devices of long ago.

The reason for narrowing a subject is to make it small enough so that you can write a full report and still have room for details (small bits of information). Details catch the attention of readers and bring the subject to life for them. But at the same time you must be careful not to make the subject too narrow. If you do, you may not have enough to write about. The "Laws of Robotics" would be too small for a good report unless you planned to tell why Isaac Asimov created the laws and where they first appeared.

With practice, you will become skillful in choosing topics that are just right for you. And sometimes, if you are alert, you will come up with ideas that no one else has thought of.

You will also become skillful in choosing a good title for your report. The title should tell as clearly as possible what the report is about. So should the title of a book or magazine article. Before they finished their reports about sponges, the members of Angie's class talked about what they would call their reports. Someone suggested "Strange Animals of the Sea." But there were two objections. First, that title does not actually tell what the report is about. How would anyone know, from that title, that the report is about sponges? Second, most sponges do live in seas, oceans, and other bodies of salt water, but a few live in lakes and other bodies of fresh water. We sometimes do say "seas" when we mean bodies of water in general, but that is not an exact use of the word. Suggestions that everyone liked were "Sponges, Strange Aquatic Animals" and "Sponges, Strange Water Dwellers." Everyone agreed, too, that "Sponges" is a good title for a report that gives general information about the subject.

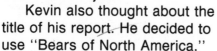

Kevin also thought about the title of his report. He decided to use "Bears of North America."

A more exact title, such as "Bears of North America and the Ones That Are in Danger of Disappearing," would be long and awkward. He planned another report with the title "Can the Grizzly Be Saved?"

THINKING IN ADVANCE

When Angie investigated the subject of sponges, she saw that she could find plenty of information about the first question, or main idea. She then discovered that there are different kinds of sponges, and she thought that this information would be important for a report. Now she had two main ideas:

1. What are sponges?
2. Are there different kinds?

Choosing a third main idea was not easy. Angie discovered that people of long ago used sponges. She also found that divers get

some of the sponges that we use. And she read an interesting legend (a story from long ago) about one kind of sponge. She did not know yet which of these main ideas to choose. She therefore wrote them all down under number 3:

3. How did people use sponges in ancient times?
    How do we get the sponges that we use?
    What are some of the legends about sponges?

In talking with her teacher about her plans, she said that she would see how much information she could find about each of the three. She hoped, though, that she could use the second one because she loved swimming and diving. And anything about diving was for her.

Kevin did some reading about bears and found that the subject would be too big if he included all the different kinds of bears in the world. He decided to narrow it to bears of North America. Because he was interested in endangered species of wildlife, he thought he would try to find out whether any of the bears of North America are in danger of disappearing. He listed these questions and talked with his teacher about his plans for his report:

1. What are the main kinds of bears in North America?

2. Where does each kind live?
3. Are any kinds of bears in danger of disappearing?

Angie and Kevin were then ready to do their research. In the same way, you will think in advance about what your main ideas may be. You cannot always know exactly. You may change your mind about what is most important and most interesting about a subject. But you will have a plan to help guide you in your search for facts.

You know that pictures, maps, charts, and other kinds of illustrations help make books and articles interesting to you. With this idea in mind, you may sometimes want to add illustrations to your report. Watch for ideas as you do your research. Toni found a picture of a beautiful sponge for his report. Another member of the class made a cover for her report and decorated it with small drawings of sponges, in fantastic shapes and colors. For a report on the voyage of the *Mayflower*, you might want to draw (or trace from a book) a map showing where the voyage began and where it ended. And for a report on an insect, you might make sketches showing how the insect looks at different stages of its life. If you took photographs when you visited a national park, Niagara Falls, a ghost mining town, or other interesting place, you might use them in a report. Whether you add illustrations depends on your topic, as well as on your own judgment.

5

Researching

(Collecting Facts or Information)

When we collect facts, or information, about a particular subject, we say that we are researching, or doing research. Where, or how, do we get the facts that we need? Television and radio programs and movies give us information. We get information by taking trips, visiting museums, and talking to people who know a great deal about a subject. We get information from newspapers, magazines, and books of many kinds.

We can also get huge amounts of information from data bases (or data banks). Data bases are collections of data, or facts, that are stored in, and can be retrieved by, computers. Different data bases contain different kinds of information. The kinds are almost endless.

Special libraries and information centers, college and university libraries, and some public and school libraries have computer terminals connected to large data bases, some of them long distances away. Users of these terminals can get information on many different subjects quickly and easily. People who have personal computers and all the equipment that is needed can use their computers to get information from certain data bases. Your chance to do research electronically may come sooner than you think, even if you do not have access to a computer terminal in a library or a personal computer for this purpose just now.

Now, as well as later, you will get many of the facts that you need from books, magazines, and other printed materials. These materials will be in a library—your school library or public library, probably both.

And you will learn how to do something that everyone, even in an electronics age, needs to know how to do. You will learn how to find your way around in a library. You will discover the "keys" that help unlock for you the great store of information that libraries contain.

To find information about bears, Kevin did not go to the librarian and say, "Have you got a book about bears?" He knew that a library has two main kinds of books that give facts or information. These are reference books and individual books about a subject. He used both kinds in his research.

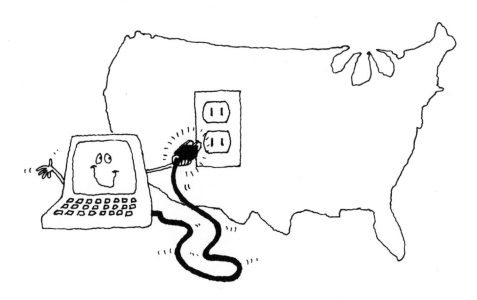

ENCYCLOPEDIAS AND OTHER REFERENCE BOOKS

Reference books are the kinds of books that people refer to (consult, or turn to) when they want to find information quickly and easily. Among the most important kinds are encyclopedias, dictionaries, atlases, biographical dictionaries, almanacs and other kinds of fact books, and indexes to periodicals (magazines and newspapers).

Reference books usually are kept in a special part of the library called the reference section. Because these books are always in demand, they usually do not circulate (that is, they cannot be borrowed for use at home). People use them at tables or desks in the reference section.

Here are some other important ideas about reference books:

1. People expect to find facts in reference books quickly and easily. And publishers of these books try to make them easy to use. If you cannot figure out for yourself how to find facts quickly in a particular reference book, ask a librarian for help. You will soon catch on and will feel at ease in the reference section.

2. People expect that the facts given in reference books will be correct. And they have learned from experience that they can indeed trust good reference books. Once in a while you may find a misprint or other mistake in even the best of books. If you are in doubt about whether a particular fact is correct, you should check it in other books.

3. There are many subjects on which experts, as well as people in general, disagree. Examples are the peaceful uses of nuclear energy, the fluoridation of drinking water, and the existence of such things as Unidentified Flying Objects. And there are many other subjects that are not completely understood, such as how the brain works and what causes certain diseases. Good reference books try to be honest and fair in giving information about such subjects. If a subject is not completely understood,

they say so, clearly. And they are careful not to mix facts with opinions. They say, for example, ''In the opinion of some experts, the reason is that. . . . Other experts think that. . . .'' Writers of reports should do the same.

4. For some subjects, you must be sure that the facts are up-to-date, as well as correct. Suppose you want to know how many women from the United States have traveled in space. You find a book that says only two women, both from the Soviet Union, have done so. Is the book wrong? The answer depends on when it was published. The first U.S. woman astronaut traveled in space in 1983. If the book was published before 1983, it could not include that information. When you are researching, you should check to find out what year a book was published. You will find this information in the copyright notice, on one of the first pages of the book. It is usually on the back of the title page (the page where the name of the book is printed in large type,

along with the names of the author or authors, and the name of the publisher of the book).

The information explosion makes it harder than ever before to keep up with the latest developments, especially in science and technology. You may not always know where to look for the latest facts on subjects that are always changing. But you will know not to use books that were published several years ago, and you will know to ask your teacher or librarian for advice. Often magazines and newspapers are the best places to look for facts that are up-to-the-minute.

Encyclopedias. Most people think of an encyclopedia as a set of books that gives information about all the different branches of knowledge. This kind of encyclopedia is called a general encyclopedia. The information about each subject is contained in an article, and the articles are usually arranged in alphabetical order. Examples of general encyclopedias are *The New Book of Knowledge*, for young people of elementary school age; the *Academic American Encyclopedia, Merit Students Encyclopedia*, and *World Book Encyclopedia*, for somewhat older students; and the *Encyclopedia Americana* and *Encyclopaedia Britannica*, for older people, in and out of school.

Some general encyclopedias are available today in electronic form (as on-line data bases and on compact disks—known as CD-ROM's—that can be hooked up to personal computers), as well as in printed form.

When you are investigating a subject, a general encyclopedia is often a good place to begin. The reason is that an encyclopedia article tries to give information about all important parts of a subject. If the article is more than just a few paragraphs, it is divided into sections. The sections have headings in bold, black type to help you see almost at a glance what each one is about.

Angie went first to a general encyclopedia and quickly found the article "Sponges" in the volume marked S. Kevin found what he needed to begin planning his report in the encyclopedia article "Bears," in the volume marked B. Later, they went back to the encyclopedia because they knew that there might be other articles, besides the main article, with information about the subject. In some cases, the most important related articles are listed at the end of the main article. But to find all the information about your subject, you should use the index. An index is an alphabetical list of all the subjects, or topics, in an encyclopedia 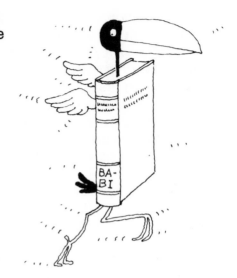 (or book), telling where to find each one. Most encyclopedias have a separate volume marked *Index*. Some have an index section at the end of each volume, as well as a separate index volume.

Some general encyclopedias publish a special volume each year called an annual, or yearbook. The purpose of these books is to help keep the encyclopedia up-to-date. They give information about the most important events of the year all around the world.

Another kind of encyclopedia is called a specialized encyclopedia because it gives information about a special subject, such as animals or birds, art, music, science and technology, or history. The *Encyclopedia of World Art* is an example. Long ago, encyclopedias often were called dictionaries. And the word "dictionary" is still used in the titles of some encyclopedias. Well-known examples are the *New Grove Dictionary of Music and Musicians* and the *Dictionary of American History*. These are multivolume encyclopedias (that is, they are sets of books).

The *Dictionary of American History* also appears in a one-volume form called the *Concise Dictionary of American History*. In either form, it is an especially good reference work on the history of the United States. And it is written in a lively and interesting style that appeals to readers of all ages.

There are one-volume reference books on sports and a great variety of other special subjects. Examples are *The Encyclopedia of Sports, The Baseball Encyclopedia*, and *The Modern Encyclopedia of Basketball.*

Dictionaries and Thesauruses. Dictionaries, in the usual sense of the term, are books that give information about words. Dictionaries tell how words are spelled, divided into syllables, and pronounced. They also explain the history and meaning or meanings. Many dictionaries give information about famous people and about places. They may also include illustrations, maps, and special charts, graphs, and tables. In fact, a good dictionary can do the work of several different reference books. If you could have only one reference book for your own, you would do well to choose a dictionary.

A thesaurus (thi SAUR us) is a special kind of word book. ("Thesaurus" comes from a Latin word that means "treasure" or "collection." The plural form is either thesauri or thesauruses.) A thesaurus lists words and gives their synonyms (words of the same or similar meaning) and antonyms (words of opposite meaning). If you overuse certain words, such as "great" or "terrific," a thesaurus is what you need to give you fresh and appropriate words. It can do wonders to increase your vocabulary and help you say exactly what you mean.

When people think of "thesaurus," they often think also of the name Roget (ro ZHAY). A thesaurus that was to become famous was compiled in the 1850s by Peter Mark Roget, a British scholar. It has gone through many editions over the years and is still in use today. There are several other word books of this kind, including a beginning thesaurus and a junior thesaurus.

Atlases and Gazetteers. An atlas is a collection of maps in book form. Some atlases cover all the continents and countries of the world. Other emphasize a certain continent or continents, such as North America or the Americas, or even a single country, such as the United States and its fifty states. Most atlases have both political maps and physical maps. Political maps show cities, towns, boundaries, and the like. Physical maps show oceans and seas and features of the land such as mountains, rivers, and lakes.

A gazetteer is a geographical dictionary. It lists countries, cities, mountains, bodies of water, and so on, and tells where they are located.

Biographical Reference Books. Many reference books give us biographical information (information about people). If we want to know about prominent living people, we can turn to the *Who's Who* reference books or to the publication called *Current Biography*. Most encyclopedias have articles about well-known people, living and dead, from all parts of the world. *Webster's New Biographical Dictionary* is a handy source of short biographies of people from around the world. The multivolume *Dictionary of American Biography* and the one-volume *Concise Dictionary of American Biography* are perhaps the best-known collections of biographies of people from the United States. There are many biographical reference books that tell about famous people in special fields, such as artists, authors, musicians, scientists, and sports figures. *The Junior Book of Authors* and *More Junior Authors* are reference books that give information about authors of books for young people.

Biographical reference books tell about the lives of many people. For that reason they usually can give only the most important facts about each person. When you are writing a report about a famous person, find out whether the library has a book-length biography of the person. Book-length biographies are kept in the main part of the library, not in the reference section.

Almanacs and Other Fact Books. Books known as almanacs are among the handiest and most popular of all books for quick reference. Examples are the *World Almanac and Book of Facts* and the *Information Please Almanac.* Books of this kind are published each year. They are jam-packed with facts about almost every subject imaginable. They also have short articles about all the states of the United States and all the countries of the world, as well as many full-color maps. Indexes and tables of contents in these books help users find what they want easily.

For reports about your state or the United States, you may need a summary of facts about population, products, weather, communications, transportation, education, and the like. Almanacs give you some of these facts. You will find many more in the *Statistical Abstract of the United States*, published each year by the United States government. Most of the states also publish fact books each year. Your librarian can tell you about these.

Almost everyone is fascinated by record-breaking facts—the biggest, the oldest, the highest, the fastest. Popular reference books that give information of this kind include the *Guinness Book of World Records* and *Famous First Facts: A Record of First Happenings, Discoveries, and Inventions in American History.* And at one time or another almost everyone thinks of a familiar quotation or saying and asks, "Who said that?" *Bartlett's Familiar Quotations* is one of several reference books that help answer that question.

Indexes to Periodicals and to World Events. Magazines and newspapers are called periodicals because they are published at certain periods of time, as daily, weekly, or monthly. Many people visit the library regularly to read the latest issues of magazines and newspapers. These are displayed in a special section of the library where there are comfortable places to sit. Earlier issues (also called back issues) of magazines usually are kept in bound volumes on shelves. Some libraries have back issues of magazines and newspapers on microfilm.

We know that magazines give us many different kinds of information. The question is, How can you find information about a particular subject in magazines without hunting through each one—an impossible job! There is a very easy way. You use certain reference books. One of these is *The Readers' Guide to Periodical Literature*. It is a subject-and-author index to all the articles that appear in more than 150 of the most popular magazines published in the United States. Some school libraries and small public libraries have the *Abridged Readers' Guide to Periodical Literature*. It is an index to a smaller number of magazines. A similar and newer guide is the *Children's Magazine Guide*. It is a subject index to articles in the most popular magazines for young people.

If you want to find magazine articles about robots, for example, you look for that subject. All the subject listings are in alphabetical order. Under the heading "Robots," you find a list of articles. Each entry gives the title of the article, the name of its author (if the author is known), the name of the magazine in which it appears, the date of the issue and the page number.

The *Children's Magazine Guide* lists articles about robots in this way:

ROBOTS: see also Toys
    Click! A Robot's Tale. Ebony Jr Aug-Sep '84 p28
    Is There a Robot in the House? One Family's Life with Topo. F.D'Ignazio. Enter Oct '84 p44-46
    Pacesetters. E.Hettich, ed. Enter Nov. 84 p24-25
    Ping-Pong Contest. Contact Oct '84 p26
    Relax: Let Robots Do the Work! Cur Sci Nov 30 '84 p11
    The Robot Invasion. S.Stuckey. Boys' Life Dec. 84 p30-33+
    Robot Patrol. P.Horowitz. K.Power Sept-Oct '84 p8
    Robotalks: A Strange Encounter in Which High Tech, Job Futures, and a Challenging World Are Debated. Career World Sep '84 p20-21
    The Robots Are Coming! Pen Pow Oct-Nov '84 p2-6
    RRRR . . . RRRRR . . . Robots! World Sep '84 p4-9
    To Market, to Market to Buy a Robot. Contact Feb '85 p23

Readers' Guide to Periodical Literature lists articles about robots in much the same way:

Robots
> *See also*
> Manipulators (Mechanism)

Tech watch [personal robotics] C. McClean, il. *Black Enterp* 15:78 Je '85

Walk this way . . . il *Pop Mech* 162:68-9 Ap '85

Industrial use
> *See also*
> American Robot Corporation
> Zymark Corporation

Composite inspection system uses robot [Boeing plant] il *Aviat Week Space Technol* 122:125 Je 17 '85

Robots and job loss [views of Anthony Patrick Carnevale] il *Futurist* 19:73 Ap '85

Robots, march on U.S. industry. D. Reed. *Read Dig* 126:188-92 Ap '85

Rubber-armed robot. S. F. Brown. il *Pop Sci* 226:28 My '85

Who said robots should work like people? W. P. Seering. il *Technol Rev* 88:58-67 Ap '85

Laboratory use

The one-armed chemist [Zymark Corp's laboratory robotic system] K. Freifeld. il *Forbes* 135 Ann Directory: 116-17 Ap 29 '85

Robots automate sample preparation. A. L. Robinson. il *Science* 227:1565-6+ Mr 29 '85

Medical use

At a California hospital, the surgeon with the steadiest hand is a robot named Ole. il por *People Wkly* 23:97 My 6 '85

Military use

Killer turtles. J. Menosky. il *Sci 85* 6:76-8 Ap '85

Space flight use

Humans still the "ultimate robots" [study at Marshall Space Flight Center] *Astronomy* 13:62+ Je '85

NASA report urges developing robotics, software for station. *Aviat Week Space Technol* 122:63 Ap 22 '85

Robots in literature

Masters and slaves, friends and enemies—tracking the literary robot. R. Sheckley. *N.Y. Times Book Rev* 90:40 Ap 21 '85

If you know that a certain author has written an article on a certain subject, you can find the article by looking under the author's name in the *Readers' Guides.* The *Children's Guide* lists articles by subject only. The listings use quite a few abbreviations, to save space. The key to the abbreviations is in the front of the guide, along with the names of the magazines that are indexed. With practice, you will find these very helpful reference books easy to use. But you should ask for help if you have trouble at first.

All the articles in certain magazines, such as *National Geographic*, are listed also in indexes that the magazines provide. These indexes are kept with the back issues of the magazines.

When you need summaries (short explanations) of world events, you can use a reference work called *Facts on File: A Weekly World News Digest with Cumulative Index.* Many libraries have *The New York Times Index* (an index to all the articles that appear in the newspaper, *The New York Times*).

You cannot learn everything about reference works all at once. As you continue to use them, you will be amazed at the number and the kinds. The reason there are so many kinds is that there are so many different kinds of facts and information.

The more you use reference books, the more discoveries you will make for yourself. In the beginning, it is helpful to have a few lessons, too. If you have not had lessons in how to use the encyclopedia and other reference books in your library, why not speak to your teacher? Everyone in your class—and your teacher, too—probably will be glad that you did.

BOOKS ABOUT
YOUR SUBJECT

To find out whether your library has individual books about your subject, or topic, you do as Kevin did. He went to the place where the library keeps a list of all the books that it owns. The books are of two main kinds—fiction (novels and storybooks) and nonfiction (books that give facts or information).

Kevin's library had the kind of list that is called a *card catalog* because the books are listed on cards that are arranged alphabetically in small drawers. Your library may have this kind, or it may have computerized catalog listings printed in book form or on *microfiche*. Microfiche are pieces of film 4 by 6 inches (10 by 15 cm). They are read on a projector. Whether cards, books, or microfiche are used, the listings are about the same.

Let us say you want to find books about robots. You do not know the name of any author who has written a book on your subject. You do not know the titles of any books about robots, either. Still, you can find out what you want to know. You go to the drawers (or books or microfiche file) and look for listings with the word "Robots" on the first line. This kind of listing is called a subject listing. Here is an example:

```
            ROBOTS
  629.8   Baldwin, Margaret
  BAL        Robots and robotics [by] Margaret Baldwin &
           Gary Pack.    Watts, 1984.
              61 p.    illus.    (A Computer-awareness first
           book)
              Describes robotics--the science of building
           robots--and gives advice on careers in that
           field.  Also defines robots and their use in
           industry, outer space, and the home.
              Bibliography: p. 57-58.
              1. Robotics  2. Robots  I. Pack, Gary
           II. T  III. Series
```

If you had known that the authors, Margaret Baldwin and Gary Pack, had written a book about robots, you could have found it by looking for the first author's last name in the drawer (or microfiche listings) marked B. This is called an author's listing. There is also a listing for the other author or authors.

And if you had known the title of the book, you could have found it by looking under the first word of the title, *Robots.* This is called a title listing. (If the title of a book begins with *The, An,* or *A,* the next word is used for the listing.)

Notice that the card tells much more than the name of the author or authors and the title of the book. It tells what company published the book and when it was published. From the card, you can find out how many pages the book has and whether it has illustrations, maps, an index, and a bibliography (a list of other books to read on the same subject). Other notes on the card tell what kinds of information you will find in the book.

The number in the upper left-hand corner of the card, 629.8, is very important. This is the class (or classification) number of the book. It helps you find the book on the library shelves.

There are so many different nonfiction books on so many different subjects that libraries must have a way of classifying them so that they can be found easily. Some libraries have their own systems, and some use a system called the Library of Congress Classification. Many others use the Dewey Decimal System, which was devised by a distinguished librarian, Melvil Dewey. It is called a decimal system because of its use of 10's. Here are the ten main classes, or subjects, of the Dewey system and their numbers:

000–099   General Works (encyclopedias, bibliographies, periodicals)
100–199   Philosophy, Psychology, Logic, Ethics (conduct)
200–299   Religion and Mythology

300–399	The Social Sciences (economics, sociology, civics, law, education, vocations, customs)
400–499	Philology (language, dictionaries, grammar)
500–599	Pure Sciences (mathematics, astronomy, physics, chemistry, geology, paleontology, biology, zoology, botany)
600–699	Useful Arts, or Technology (medicine, engineering, agriculture, home economics, business, radio, television, aeronautics)
700–799	The Arts (architecture, sculpture, painting, music, photography, recreation)
800–899	Literature (novels, poetry, plays, criticism)
900–999	History, Geography, Travel

Each of these ten main classes is divided into ten smaller subject fields. In the main class 600–699, for example, the divisions would be 610, 620, and so on, up to 690. And each of these divisions can be divided again and again by using a decimal point after the first three numbers. Books about certain kinds of aircraft are given the class number 629.1, and books about automobiles, 629.2. Books about robots have the number 629.8, as you can see on the card.

All books on the same subject have the same class number, and there may be many books on the same subject by different authors. If there are, the library may add a letter or letters below the class number—for example, B or BAL. This is the initial (or the first letters) of the author's last name. The class number plus the author's initial or letters is known as the call number. Books are arranged on the shelves according to their class numbers and then, in alphabetical order, according to the authors' initials or letters.

When you find a listing for your subject, you should write down the call number, along with the name of the author and the title of the book. You are then ready to go to the shelves to look

for it. Usually the shelves are plainly marked 100's, 200's, and so on. And the call number of each book is marked on its spine (the part of book that faces you when it is sitting on the shelf). Perhaps you will find other books on your subject, as well as the one you were looking for.

If you do not find listings for your subject, try to think of other subjects that might include it. Angie found no cards with the word "Sponges," and the librarian suggested that she look for subject cards beginning with the word "Marine" or "Ocean" or "Sea." Under those words, she found some cards, and she studied the information on each one. Then she made a note of the call numbers, authors, and titles of two of the books. She got the books and quickly found out whether they had information that would help her with her report. This is how she did it:

1. She turned to the page in the front of the book that said *Contents* or *Table of Contents*. She looked down the list of contents. In one book she found that there was a part entitled "Sponges," beginning on a certain page. The table of contents in the other book listed nothing on sponges, but Angie knew what else to do.

2. She turned to the back of the book, to the page that said *Index*. She looked down the alphabetized list of subjects, or topics, for the word "Sponges" and found that the book gave some information about sponges on several different pages.

When you have found books on your subject, you should do as Angie did. Take them to a table where you can sit comfortably, and use the contents page and the index to find out whether they have the information you need.

Contents

What is a volcano?	4
Mighty eruptions	6
Active volcanoes	8
Underwater volcanoes	10
Rivers of fire	12
Bombs, dust and ash	14
Hot springs and geysers	16
Vesuvius	18
Krakatoa!	20
Mount St. Helens	22
Predicting eruptions	24
Useful volcanoes	26
Volcanoes in space	28
Glossary	30
Fascinating Facts	31
Index	32

The contents page for *Volcanoes* by David Lambert shows the kinds of information in the book.

Index

acid lava 14, 30
Aconcagua 31
active volcanoes 4, 8, 9
Anak Krakatoa 21
Ash 4, 14, 18, 23

basalt rock 12
batholiths 6, 7, 30
borax 26, 27
bread-crust bomb 15

caldera 15, 30
cone 4, 5, 10, 12, 15, 22
crater 4, 12, 14, 15, 22
crust 4, 6, 7, 11
crustal plates 6, 7, 8, 9, 11, 30

diamonds 26, 27
dormant volcanoes 4
dried mud bomb 15
dykes 4, 5, 30

earthquake shocks 25
earthquakes 18
electricity supply 27
explosive volcanoes 14, 30

fissures 12, 29
fumaroles 17

geysers 16, 17, 30
gold 26

granite 6, 26
guyots 10, 30

Hawaii 12, 15, 25, 31
Heimaey 14
Herculaneum 18, 19
hot springs 17

Iceland 11, 12, 14, 17
igneous rock 26, 30
infrared photography 24
Io 29

Jupiter 29

Kilauea 25
Krakatoa 8, 9, 20, 21

lava 4, 5, 7, 9, 12, 14, 29, 30
lava ridge 11

magma 4, 5, 14, 20, 24, 25, 27, 30
mantle 6, 9, 11
Mauna Loa 12
Mid-Atlantic Ridge 8, 9, 11
Moon 29
Mount Etna 8, 25
Mount Fuji 4
Mount St. Helens 8, 22, 23
Mount Vesuvius 4, 8, 9, 18, 19

Old Faithful 17
Olympus Mons 28

peridots 26, 27
Pompeii 18, 19
pumice 23, 30

quiet volcano 30

ridges 6, 7, 10, 31
Ring of Fire 8, 9

Santorini 31
seamounts 10, 31
seismograph 24, 25
sills 4, 5, 31
solfataras 17
spreading ridge 31
Stromboli 12, 13
subduction zone 7
Surtsey 11

Tambora 31
tiltmeter 24, 25
transform faults 10
tremors 24, 25
tsunami 20, 21

Vesuvius 18
volcanic bombs 14, 15, 20
volcanic dust 14, 15
volcanoes in space 28, 29
Vulcano Island 31
Vulcanus 31

The index for *Volcanoes* by David Lambert is a complete guide to where information can be found in the book.

Biographies usually are kept together on their own shelves, separate from other nonfiction books, and are arranged alphabetically according to the subjects' last names. (The subjects are the persons that the biographies are about.) But libraries may have different ways of marking the spines of these books and arranging them. Your librarian will tell you where these books are in your library and how they are arranged.

Books of fiction, too, are kept together on their shelves. They have F or Fict on their spines, and they are arranged alphabetically according to the last name of the authors.

Information about many subjects, such as individual national parks, state parks, and state emblems, often is published in the form of leaflets, or pamphlets. Some libraries have collections of pamphlets, clippings, and the like. Usually these are arranged by subject and are kept in a file called a vertical file. You might find pamphlets about your subject there. If not, the librarian probably could show you how to find the address of the National Park Service or of the department of your state government or other agency that publishes the information and sends it, usually free of charge, to people who ask for it. The library may also have films, filmstrips, records, or cassettes that would help you with reports on some topics.

OTHER SOURCES OF INFORMATION

Members of Kevin's class found that television programs often give information or spark ideas for reports. Kevin himself was the class "specialist" on wildlife programs. He checked the program listings and alerted everyone to what was coming up. Angie did the same for programs about deep-sea diving and underwater exploration. She had the help of another member of the class who was especially interested in robots. He was thrilled by programs that show how robot submarines and other devices are used to explore the ocean floor and to hunt for sunken ships of long ago. Other members of the class watched for programs that feature life in faraway places and other subjects of special interest to them. You, too, can search the listings for programs that might help you.

Toni went to the Museum of Natural History to see whether he could find information there about sponges. To his surprise, a museum guide led him to a place where a few sponges were displayed. He remembered then that he had seen them before but had never paid attention to what they were. Usually he had been most interested in the dinosaurs. He went then to the shop in the museum to see whether he might find pictures of sponges on postcards, or books or pamphlets about sponges.

Museums are an especially good place to look for information. If you live in a city, you probably know about the larger museums, such as museums of art, natural history, and science and industry. Perhaps you have visited them. Perhaps you have visited museums for young people, too. But you might be surprised to know how many smaller museums there are, specializing in different subjects. To find out about these, look under the heading "Museums" in your classified telephone directory.

Smaller cities and towns have interesting and important museums, too. Besides art museums, there may be museums devoted to state or local history, pioneer life, native American peoples, or any number of other special subjects such as fossils, rocks and minerals, mining, farm life, watches and clocks, automobiles, or trolley cars. Some of these museums may have pamphlets or guidebooks, and the dispays usually have labels that give interesting bits of information. One way to find out about museums in the part of the country where you live is to use a reference book called *The Official Museum Directory.* It lists all kinds of museums, large and small, in all parts of the country.

People who know a great deal about a subject are another good source of information, and they are usually pleased to be asked to share their knowledge. For reports on careers, or vocations, why not talk with someone who does a kind of work that interests you? It might be a newspaper reporter, a police officer, a shopkeeper, a health care worker, a farmer, or a politician. For reports on industries and products, think about the different kinds of businesses and factories in your community. Do you know exactly what products a certain factory makes, how they are made, and how they are used? A visit to a factory and a talk with someone there might make an interesting subject for a report.

People who travel a great deal might give you information about such subjects as the pyramids of Egypt, the wildlife of Kenya, or the Amazon jungles. For information about the most important wildflowers of your state, you might talk to a member of the local garden club. Dog breeders or trainers could tell you about their specialties. Historical societies, public libraries, or other agencies sometimes have oral history projects, in which people tape-record their memories of earlier times. These projects may give information about a variety of topics.

When you seek information from anyone, it is polite to ask for the privilege of an interview and to write a thank-you note afterward. You should go to the interview prepared with questions about what you want to know. And you should take notes.

6

Taking Notes

Before Kevin started his research, he wrote each of his questions on a separate sheet in a good-sized notebook. He chose a notebook with a spiral binding—the kind from which you can remove sheets when you no longer need them. This is a good plan for you to follow. Take the notebook with you to the library, and you will be all ready to take notes of facts that you need for your report.

Some researchers like to take notes on small cards called index cards. Cards are handy for big jobs, when the researcher expects to have a large number of notes. But for school reports you will probably find a notebook easy to use and safer, since cards are easily scattered and lost.

When you have found the part of an encyclopedia article, book, or magazine article that has facts that you need, follow this plan:

1. Read the paragraph or paragraphs once, looking for answers to your questions. Then go back and read again just those sentences that help answer your questions. *Do not write anything yet.* Just think carefully about what you have read and how you will express the ideas in your own words.

The New Book of Knowledge, 1985, Vol. 2.
"Bears." Pages 104-107
"The World of the Brown Bear," National
Geog. World, Jan. '84. Pages 18-24
Graham, Ada and Frank. Bears in
the Wild. NY: Delacorte Press.
1981. Pages 85, 88, 42.

Notes

Bears of North America

1. What are the main Kinds?
  ② Big brown bears
    Two Kinds, Alaskan brown bears and grizzlies New Book of Know. p.107
    Once thought to be two different species, now Graham, p.88
    known to be close kin of a single species
           New Book of Knowl., p.107
  ③ Polar bears Graham, p.92

  ① American black bears
    called black but not all black Graham, 44 New Book of Knowl., p.105
    smallest of the three Kinds

53—

2. Put a slip of paper in the book to mark your place. *Close the book*, and write short notes—as short as you possibly can—in the spaces under the questions to help you remember what you have read.

3. Open the book, and check to be sure that you have written names, dates, and other facts correctly.

4. If there are other parts of the same article or book that may help answer one or more of your questions—and if you use other books—follow exactly the same steps: Read once, looking for facts that you need. Read again, and decide how you will express the ideas in your own words. Close the book. Take notes. Open the book and check what you have written.

5. When you finish taking notes from a book, always remember to do one more thing: At the top of your sheet of paper, write the name of the book in which you found the facts and the numbers of the pages on which you found them. Notice that Kevin made notes on information he found in an encyclopedia, a book, and a magazine article.

7

Giving Credit to Others

Everyone is welcome to use the information in books, magazines, newspapers, and the like. That is what information is for—to be used. But when we use information prepared by other people, it is only fair to give them credit for it.

Giving credit to others is an important part of writing a report. It is also interesting and easy to do. The first step is to keep a careful record of the books and articles that you use. You do this when you are taking notes. Then you prepare a list, called a *bibliography* (see pages 74-77), and hand it in along with your report.

We need to say one more thing about giving credit to others. It is true that everyone is welcome to use the information in books. But no one may copy from a book and pretend that what was copied is his or her own work. Often you find sentences or expressions that you like very much and want to use, word for

word. You may do so if you show clearly that the words are not your own. Follow this plan:

1. Put quotation marks around any expression or sentences that you copy when you are taking notes.

2. Be sure to copy exactly. People who write articles and books usually are pleased to be quoted, but not to be misquoted.

3. If you use an expression or sentence that is not your own in a report, put quotation marks around it and tell who wrote it or where you found it. (Quotations can help to make a report interesting. Notice that Angie used a description of sponges that she found in *The New Book of Knowledge*.)

Besides giving credit, there are other reasons for listing the books and articles that you use. The readers of your report may want to find out more about the subject, and your list will help them know where to look. They also may want to know where you got the information so that they may judge for themselves whether you used reliable sources—books and articles that are likely to give correct and up-to-date information.

8

Making an Outline

There is one more important step to take before you start to write your report. That step is making an outline. It will be easy because all the other steps have led you directly to it. And the writing of the report will follow easily from the outline.

WHAT YOU MAY KNOW
ABOUT OUTLINING

Perhaps you know something about outlining. In your reading classes—and in social studies, science, and other subjects—you may have had practice in finding the main idea in a paragraph or paragraphs in your textbooks. When you find the first main idea and are sure you understand it, you make a note of it in your own words. Next, you find the details (facts, or ideas) that help explain the main idea, and you list these details under it. Then you go ahead, finding other main ideas and the details that go with them.

When you study an assignment in this way, usually you can say, "I understand what I have read." And a week later—or a month or even a year later—you are likely to remember. The reason you understand and remember is that you have *organized the ideas.*

To organize means simply "to sort things out and to put together the things that belong together." That is what you do when you outline. You sort out the main ideas, and you put with them the facts or ideas that belong with them, in this way:

A. First main idea
   1. Fact or idea that belongs with the first main idea
   2. Another fact or idea that belongs with it
   3. Still another fact or idea that belongs with it
B. Next main idea
   1. Fact or idea that belongs with this main idea
   2. Another fact or idea that belongs with it
   3. Still another

WHAT YOU MAY NOT KNOW

Of course, there is nothing magic about outlining. It will help you only if you know what you are doing and why. Sometimes people say they have trouble. The trouble with outlining—if there is trouble—starts at the beginning. It starts with too much tiresome writing of long notes. When you outline something you are reading or studying, you do three things:

1. You read.
2. You think about, and perhaps discuss, what you have read.
3. You write, making short notes in a special form called an outline.

By far the most important parts are reading and thinking. By reading and thinking, you get the ideas sorted out and organized

in your mind. You write only enough to help remind yourself of what you have read.

Another way to think about outlining is this: If you make a correct outline, you discover the plan, or outline, that the author made before starting to write the material that you are studying.

Why do people who write books and articles about history, sports, art, science, geography, health, and other subjects begin by making an outline?

One reason is that authors cannot tell everything about a subject. They have to decide what parts to put into certain books or articles and in what order the parts should go. Another reason— even more important—is that authors have to think about their readers. After all, the purpose of books or articles is to give readers important and interesting information about a subject. Usually, the harder authors work at thinking and organizing before they begin to write, the easier their books will be to understand. Outlines keep them on the track, so that they will not switch from one main idea to another and back again, in a way that would be confusing to readers.

Think about the books and articles that you have enjoyed most. They seemed almost to talk to you. The reason is that the authors spent a great deal of time thinking about you—and about how to organize ideas and to "talk on paper" so that the ideas would be interesting and clear to you.

WHY OUTLINING YOUR REPORT WILL BE EASY

You probably understood why Angie and Kevin wrote down certain questions after they had done some investigating of their topics. They were thinking about the main ideas, and they were beginning to organize, or outline, their reports.

Before they started to do their research and take notes, they wrote each question on a separate sheet in their notebooks. You probably understood, too, why they did this. When they found facts or ideas that helped answer their questions, they would have plenty of room to write notes below each one. In this way, they were making a rough outline in advance. And the next step—making a good, clear outline—was easy.

THE FORM TO USE

The parts of an outline may be numbered (or lettered) in different ways. You may use capital letters (A, B, C, and so on) for the main ideas, and numerals (1, 2, 3) for the facts or ideas that are written down under the main ideas. Kevin used this plan. Or you may use roman numerals (I, II, III) and capital letters, as Angie did.

You may write full sentences, as Angie did. This kind of outline is called a *sentence outline*. Or you may write phrases (little

Sponges — Outline

I. Sponges are strange animals that live in seas and other bodies of water.
   A. People once thought sponges were plants because they seem more like plants than animals.
   B. Now scientists know that sponges are animals because of the way they get their food.
   C. Sponges strain food from water that pours into them through holes, or pores, in their bodies.

II. Scientists classify natural sponges by their skeletons. There are also synthetic sponges.
   A. One kind of natural sponge has a skeleton of lime or chalk.
   B. Another kind has a glassy skeleton.
   C. The kind of natural sponge that we use has a skeleton made up mostly of fibers called spongin.
   D. We also use sponges made of rubber or other substances.

III. The natural sponges that we use come from parts of the Mediterranean and Caribbean seas.
   A. Tarpon Springs, Florida, is one place where sponges are harvested.
   B. In shallow water, people use boats to get sponges.
   C. Divers gather sponges in deeper water.

Outline

Bears of North America

A. The three main kinds
   1. American black bears
   2. Big brown bears (Alaskan brown bears and grizzlies)
   3. Polar bears
B. Where each kind lives
   1. Black bears in most wooded parts of Canada, the United States, and northern Mexico.
   2. Alaskan brown bears in southern Alaska
   3. Grizzlies once all over western North America, now mainly in Canada and Alaska
   4. Polar bears in the Arctic
C. Kinds in danger of disappearing
   1. Polar bears once in danger, now protected from sports hunters by law
   2. Grizzlies in danger of disappearing south of Canada

groups of words—not full sentences), as Kevin did. This kind of outline is called a *topic outline.*

If your teacher has requested that you follow a specific plan, use it. Otherwise, you may choose the form that seems best to you. Sometimes you may make a sentence outline, and sometimes a topic outline.

CHANGING YOUR NOTES INTO OUTLINE FORM

To do almost anything well, you need practice. The same is true of changing your notes into outline form. With practice, you will soon do it easily and well. Notice what Kevin did.

The first question in his notes was "What are the main kinds of bears in North America?" For his outline, he changed this to the short phrase "The three main kinds" and listed the kinds under it. His next question was "Where does each kind live?" He changed this to "Where each kind lives" for his outline. Before listing the points under each main topic, he went over his notes carefully. He struck out notes that he did not need, and he rearranged some of the points.

Angie chose to make a sentence outline. Otherwise, she worked in the same way that Kevin did.

Here are some points to check on every outline:

1. Put a period after each letter or number.
2. Place the letters or numbers and the periods in a straight line, up and down.
3. Capitalize the first word of each main idea and each idea under it.
4. If you are making a sentence outline, put a period at the end of each sentence. But if you are making a topic outline, do not use periods at the end.

You should hand in your outline with your report, even though your teacher may not have asked for it. There are good reasons for handing in the outline, especially when you are learning how to prepare reports.

One reason is that you have worked on the outline and have tried to make it correct and attractive-looking. It deserves to be seen.

Another reason, as you know by this time, is that outlining is one of the most important parts of preparing a report. When you begin to prepare reports and to do other kinds of writing in school, *you* become a writer, or author. You work in the same way that all writers work. When you make a good, clear outline and then follow it in writing, your readers will find your report clear and easy to understand. And even if your work is praised, you will still want to know how to make it better. Seeing your outline will make it easier for your teacher to help you.

OTHER IMPORTANT IDEAS ABOUT OUTLINING

When you have had some experience in writing reports, you will probably be on your own to follow all the steps to the point where you make your outline. You will be pleased to discover how much you can do by yourself. One of the good things about preparing reports is that it helps you learn how to figure things out for yourself—to work independently without being told every little thing to do. Of course, you will have problems occasionally. Everyone does. When you are not sure about your outline, do not waste time in worrying. Ask your teacher for a conference, and go prepared to state the problem as best you can.

Sometimes you may write reports about trips you have taken, experiments you have performed, delicious dishes you have prepared, or other subjects for which you do not need to search for information—except in your mind. It is very important to make outlines for reports of this kind, too.

Many times you will give reports orally instead of writing them. Is it important to make a good, clear outline of an oral report? Absolutely! The reasons for outlining before you speak are the same as the reasons for outlining before you write. Speakers, like writers, know that the harder they work organizing what they want to say, the better they will say it. And the better they say it, the more their listeners will get out of it.

9

Writing Your Report

Up to this time you have been learning about all the things a writer does before actually starting to write a report (or an article or book that gives information). Now you are ready for the very last steps:

1. You will write the first draft (the first copy).
2. You will correct and improve the first draft.
3. You will make a neat final copy of your report, your outline, and your bibliography.
4. You will put everything together, perhaps with a cover and illustrations.

WRITING THE FIRST DRAFT

Your first draft can be written in pencil on almost any kind of paper. It is a good idea to write only on every other line so that you will have plenty of room to make corrections.

You should have your outline before you when you start to write. It shows how many paragraphs you will have and what you will tell about in each paragraph. Because of all the thinking and organizing you have done, you probably will be able to write rapidly.

Do not think especially about spelling, punctuation, and capitalization at this time. Think mainly about what you are saying and about how to express each idea as clearly and as briefly as possible.

CORRECTING AND IMPROVING THE FIRST DRAFT

When they finish the first draft, some writers like to begin at once to correct and improve their work. Others prefer to put the first draft away for a while and then come back to it. They believe that in this way they can look at their work with a fresh mind. They can look at it almost as if it were not their own work, but something that someone else had written. Most of us do find it easier to discover mistakes and faults in other people's work than to discover our own mistakes.

Whichever way you choose to correct and improve your draft, you will do best if you have a plan for checking. In that way you will not be looking for everything all at once and seeing nothing. The following plan can be very helpful. Follow each step as well as you can. When you meet a problem or have a question that you cannot answer by yourself, make a note. Then, when you finish checking, ask your teacher for a brief conference to talk over the problems.

Sponges

Sponges are animals. They live in seas and other bodies of water, but they are very strange. animals. People once thought they were plants. They have no head or mouth or feet. But scientists now agree that they are animals because of the way they get

but are made of rubber or other substances.

~~Sponges made in factories are not as good as natural sponges.~~

Bears of North America

~~There~~ Three

~~They are three~~ kinds of bears Live. N
                                  ^   in north

America. They are ~~the~~ American black bears, ~~the~~

                              polar   Big
big brown bears, and ~~the~~ ~~polar~~ bears. ~~The big~~

                                    Alaskan
brown bears are of two kinds, the ~~alaskan~~ brown

              grizzly
bear and the ~~glizzly~~ bear.

A PLAN FOR CHECKING

First check your spelling, punctuation, and capitalization. How do you check your spelling? You look carefully at each word. If you are not sure that a word is correct, try to look it up by yourself in a dictionary. If you have trouble, make a note to remind yourself to discuss the problem with your teacher.

Notice that Angie left a letter out of the word "sci en tist." She discovered the mistake because she had learned to point to each syllable when checking her spelling, especially of long words.

Angie also wrote "though" when she meant "thought." Kevin wrote "they" when he meant "there." Sometimes we write one word when we mean another. Watch especially for this kind of mistake.

How do you check your punctuation and capitalization? To help yourself find an answer, ask yourself these questions:

> What rules of punctuation have I studied in my English (or language arts) class?
> What rules of capitalization have I studied?

When you have answered these questions, you will know exactly what you should check.

Next, read each of your sentences carefully. Ask yourself these questions:

> Is each sentence a complete sentence?
> Is the meaning of each sentence clear?
> Do all the sentences in a paragraph go well together?
> Can I see a way to improve any sentence?

Notice Kevin's first paragraph. Each sentence is complete. The meaning of each one is very clear. The reader will find out at once how many kinds of bears there are in North America. Next, the reader will want to know what the kinds are. Kevin gives that information in the very next sentence.

When Kevin was talking with his teacher about his first draft, the teacher complimented him on finding the mistake that he had made in writing *they* for *there*. Then the teacher helped him discover that his sentences began in similar ways—"There are. . . . They are. . . ."

"The beginnings are too much alike, aren't they?" said Kevin. "They're monotonous, like the sentences we talked about in English class the other day."

He decided to change his first sentence. Then he read the first and second sentences one after the other and agreed that the change improved the paragraph.

Usually English class is the place where you learn how to improve your sentences, just as Kevin had learned in his English class about monotonous beginnings. The report he was writing was for his science class. But he remembered a dialogue that members of his class sometimes repeated when they were studying rules of capitalization and punctuation and ways of improving sentences. The dialogue went this way:

Teacher: Why are we studying this in English class?
Class: To use in all our writing for all our classes.

Everyone always laughed, but everyone understood and remembered—most of the time.

Last, remember that a report must give information fairly, as well as correctly. Facts must not be confused with opinions. Check your sentences to see whether each one is an honest statement of fact, not an opinion stated as though it were a fact.

Notice that in her first draft Angie crossed out the sentence "Sponges made in factories are not as good as natural sponges." She did so because her teacher helped her understand that this sentence expresses an opinion, not a fact. Instead of taking the sentence out, she might have written, "Some people think that sponges made in factories are not as good as natural sponges. Other people disagree."

For practice, read the following pairs of sentences. Can you tell which one in each pair is not a statement of fact?

1. Abraham Lincoln was a famous President of the United States.
   Abraham Lincoln was our most famous President.
2. Florida has a better climate than any other state.
   The climate of Florida is generally mild and sunny.
3. The United States has many good scientists.
   The United States has the best scientists in the world.
4. The airplane is the best way to travel.
   Many people think the airplane is the best way to travel.
5. Wheat is one of the important crops grown in the United States.
   Wheat is the most important crop grown in the United States.

MAKING A NEAT FINAL COPY OF YOUR REPORT

Now you have come to the very last step in preparing a report—making the copy that you will present to your readers. It is true that if you have a personal computer, you can use it to write your report, even as you can do some research by computer, if you have the additional equipment that is needed. And you could send your report directly to your teacher, if both you and your teacher have the equipment needed to send and receive copy by telephone. Some reporters write on computers at home and send their articles directly to their newspaper offices. And some authors compose their books on computers and send the copy directly by phone to their publishers, without ever touching pen and paper or typewriters.

Perhaps you, too, will write electronically someday, even if you cannot do so just now. In the meantime, remember that

everyone still needs to know how to produce handwriting that is neat and easily read. Handwriting and handwritten work did not go out of style after typewriters were invented. Computers with printers and word-processing software are not likely to do away with the need for good, clear handwritten work, either.

If you have been doing different kinds of writing, you know how your teacher wishes you to arrange your papers. You will know where to put the heading (your name and the date), the title, and all the rest. But if you have not been given instructions, you may follow these suggestions:

1. Plan your paper so that the writing fits nicely on the page, almost as if it were a picture in a frame. What you write is the picture. The white space all around is the frame.

2. Write with a pen. A pencil is fine for everyday work, but a pen is required for all writing that you present to other people.
3. Be sure that your handwriting is neat and easy to read.
4. Put the title on the first line. Do not underline it unless it happens to be the title of a book, newspaper, or magazine. Do not put quotation marks around it unless it is a quotation. Ask your teacher if you are in doubt.
5. Skip a line after the title, and start writing on the next line.
6. Indent the first word of each paragraph.
7. Keep the left margin very straight. Keep the right margin as straight as you can.
8. Remember to number the pages when you have more than one page.

Your list of sources is called a bibliography. The word is a long one, but it means simply "a list of books or articles on a certain subject." Your bibliography should be copied on a separate page.

There are different ways of listing articles and books in a bibliography. Some persons prefer one way, and some prefer another. If your teacher has shown you one way, you will use it. Otherwise, you may use the plan that Kevin used. We shall see first how to list books, then how to list articles from encyclopedias and magazines.

In listing a book, you give the same facts, in general, that are given on the card or microfiche in the library catalog. Here is the order in which you write the facts:

1. The full name of the author or authors (with last name first)
2. The title of the book
3. The city where the book was published. (Usually this is

Bears of North America

Bibliography

1. "Bears," <u>The New Book of Knowledge</u>, 1985, Volume 2. Pages 104-107.

2. Graham, Ada and Frank. <u>Bears in the Wild</u>. New York : Delacorte Press, 1981.

3. "The World of the Brown Bear," <u>National Geographic World</u>, January, 1984. Pages 18-24.

not on the card or microfiche, but you can find it easily on one of the first pages of the book.)
4. The name of the publisher
5. The year of publication

Capitalization and punctuation are important in listing. Check yourself carefully on these points:

1. Put a comma after the author's (or each author's) last name and a period at the end of the complete name (or names).
2. Capitalize the first word and all other important words in the title of the book, underline the title, and put a period at the end.
3. Put a colon (:) after the city where the book was published, put a comma after the name of the publisher, and put a period after the year of publication.

In listing an article from an encyclopedia or a magazine, you use a plan that is somewhat different from the plan used in listing a book. You can see why. An encyclopedia usually has many different volumes, and each volume has hundreds of articles. Magazines are issued weekly or monthly. Each issue has many different articles, written by different authors. Sometimes the name of the author of a magazine article is given, and sometimes it is not.

Keep the listing as simple as possible. Follow the plan that Kevin used if your teacher has not suggested a different way:

1. For an encyclopedia article, begin with the title of the article. Put quotation marks around it. Next, give the name of the encyclopedia, underlined, the year it was published (you find the year on one of the first pages of the first volume), and the number of the volume. Then add the page numbers of the article.

2. For a magazine article, begin with the name of the author (last name first) if the author is given. If no author is given, begin with the title of the article, in quotation marks. Then give the name of the magazine, underlined, and the date the issue was published (month and year, or month, day, and year). Last, give the page number or numbers of the article.

When you make the final copy of your bibliography, you arrange the entries (listings) in alphabetical order, according to the first important word in each entry. In Kevin's bibliography, for example, the entries are arranged in alphabetical order according to the words *Bears, Graham,* and *World.*

The final copies of your report, bibliography, and outline go together, along with illustrations, perhaps. Sometimes you may decide to design a cover, to make a complete "package." Present your work to your teacher and classmates with confidence that you have done your best. And start thinking about how you will improve your work in your next report.

10

Book Reviews

and Reports

The purpose of the first chapters of this book is to help you learn how to do a kind of writing that probably will be useful to you all your life.

This chapter is quite different, although its purpose is to help you with something that not only will be useful to you but will bring you great pleasure all your life. This chapter is about ways of discovering and sharing the good things in books.

Have you found some books that you liked very much—books that became friends? Books that took you on adventures or cheered you or taught you new and interesting things?

If you have found some books that interest you, you are fortunate. If not, sooner or later you are sure to find quite a few. Some of these will be fiction (books about imaginary characters and events), and others will be nonfiction.

When you find a book that you like, usually you want to talk about it—to share your pleasure with others. When you tell your classmates about what you have read, you help them find books that they may like. And they, in turn—by sharing with you—may help you make interesting discoveries.

There are many ways of discovering and sharing books. Some teachers and their classes prefer certain ways, and others prefer other ways. One way is through reporting on, or reviewing, books.

GIVING ORAL REVIEWS

When you see an unfamiliar book, the first questions that pop into your mind usually are "What is it about? Is it really good?" The answers to those questions can help you decide whether you might like to read it. Those questions, then, give you clues about what to say when you are telling your classmates about a book.

Here is a plan that you might follow:

1. Give the title and the author, and show the book if you have it with you.
2. Tell very briefly (in just a few sentences) what the book is about.
3. Read a short part aloud, or tell about an especially interesting part.
4. Read, or tell, just enough to make the listeners want to know more. Never, never give away the surprises in the book or spoil in any way the listeners' desire to read the book themselves.
5. Show some of the pictures, if there are any.
6. Give your opinion of the book, or tell why you think your listeners would like it.

KEEPING
READING RECORDS

Some people keep reading records all their lives. These records often are journals, or diaries, in which they jot down ideas that they want to remember because the ideas have a special meaning for them. These ideas may be something that the author of a book has said or something said by a story character.

Many young people keep records of what they read during their school years. Because there are many ways of keeping reading records, teachers and their classes often discuss different ways and choose one each year. If your class has chosen a certain form, you will use that, of course.

If you are looking for an idea, you might like the plan that Juan's class used. All the members of the class had individual sheets, like the one on the next page, that they kept in a loose-leaf notebook. As they read books during the year, they recorded those books on their sheets, listing author, title, kind of book, and date. The big notebook kept the sheets safe, so that no one's record was lost. Everyone enjoyed looking through the notebook to see what the others were reading.

WRITING REVIEWS, NOTES, AND COMMENTS

At the beginning of the school year, the members of a class talked about books they had read during the summer. Each one agreed to select one book and write a few sentences about it. They had not yet decided how they would handle their written reviews during the year.

A Book Review, or Report

Wes wrote about a book that he and his friends at camp had enjoyed reading. He wrote the review on a card because he thought it would be a good idea for the class to keep a box of book review cards, as the members of his class at another school had done the year before. Whenever anyone read a book, he or she would prepare a brief review, write it on a card, and put it into

Reading Record of _Juan Santos_

Author	Title	Kind of Book	Date Read
White, E.B.	The Trumpet of the Swan	Story	June 13
Lambert, Mark	50 Facts About Robots	Science	June 21
Hoke, Helen	Jokes, Jokes, Jokes	Fun	June 30
Seuss, Dr.	Thidwick: The Big-Hearted Moose	Story	July 9
Stoddard, Edward	Magic	How-To-Do	July 30
Edmonds, Walter	The Matchlock Gun	Story	Aug. 6

Frommer, Harvey. Baseball's Hall of Fame. New York: Franklin Watts, 1985.

This book tells all about what you can see at the National Baseball Hall of Fame and Museum at Cooperstown, New York, and it explains how players and others are elected to the Hall of Fame. There are biographies of 50 of the members. Each one is packed with interesting information about the person and his record. All the members of the Hall of Fame are listed at the end of the book. —Wes Benson.

the box. When others read the book, they would add their comments on the back of the card—in one sentence, each. Each comment was signed.

All the members of the class liked the idea. They agreed that they would keep a box of book review cards. Someone suggested that they might arrange the cards in groups to show the kinds of books reviewed, such as these:

Adventure and Mystery	Science Fiction
Biography	Sports
Science and Nature	Tales and Legends

Fran, like other members of the class, had written her review on a sheet of paper. She said she would copy it onto a card for the book review box.

Miss Pickerell and the War of the Computers
by Dora Pantell

Had the computer that sent prices to the supermarket gone mad? Or were computers at war with each other, as Miss Pickerell's nephew said they might be? Anyway, prices were up 800 percent, and people were desperate. Miss P. decided that something must be done. So she left Nancy Agatha the cow, Pumkins the cat, and the new puppy Sampson in the care of kind Mr. Kettelson and flew off by helicopter to the Computer Processing Center. What she learned about Computers and how she helped solve the mystery will amaze you.

Fran Pettit

83—

The written reviews, or reports, are much like oral reviews. Wes wrote about a book that gives information. Fran wrote about a storybook. Both of them followed this general plan:

1. Give the author and the title. (It is a good idea also to give place of publication, name of publisher, and the date, just as Wes did.)
2. Tell very briefly what the book is about.
3. Mention an interesting part, but never tell too much, and never reveal the surprises in the book.
4. Give your opinion of the book.

Sometimes you may be expected to write book reviews or reports that are longer than the ones Wes and Fran wrote. If so, your teacher probably will tell you what plan to use.

Notes About Favorite Authors

Nell wrote about one of her favorite authors and about some of her favorite books, too. She suggested that the class might keep a favorite-author file, as a well as a book review file.

The members of the class agreed, and they talked about ways of finding information about authors. These are some of the ways they mentioned:

1. Sometimes a book jacket gives information about the author.
2. Some books have a special page, usually at the end, telling about the author.
3. There are reference books about authors, such as *Junior Book of Authors, More Junior Authors,* and *Current Biography.*
4. Most encyclopedias have articles about the lives of famous authors.

Nell Teng

Laura Ingalls Wilder

Mrs. Wilder was born in a log cabin in Wisconsin. She traveled with her family by covered wagon through Minnesota and Kansas and other places. The story of her life is told in her books. Everything in them is very real, and they are my favorites. Mrs. Wilder died at the age of ninety at her home in the Ozarks of Missouri. These are some of her books:

Little House in the Big Woods
Little House on the Prairie
Farmer Boy
On the Banks of Plum Creek

5. There are also book-length biographies of some authors.

Probably you can think of other ways of finding out about good
books and sharing your discoveries. To get ideas, all you need is
a start. Once you have a start, one thing usually leads to another
in surprising and delightful ways.

Basic Tools for

Young Researchers—

A Quick Review

Mechanics and plumbers, potters and sculptors depend on certain kinds of basic tools. In somewhat the same way, workers in the information industry have basic tools, which they use in researching, or finding information. Experienced researchers know all about these tools. You, as a young researcher, will discover and learn to use these tools little by little.

Chapter 5 of this book explains and gives the names of some of the best-known research tools, or reference books. Here is a brief review, with additional help and hints:

1. General encyclopedias. Articles in general encyclopedias, as you have learned, often get you off to a good start because they give information about all the important parts of a subject. General encyclopedias can also help you in other ways:

(a) They can help you find books about your subject. In some encyclopedias, such as the *World Book Encyclopedia*, you find lists of related books at the end of certain articles. *The New Book of Knowledge* has a separate *Reading Guide* (a paperback book), which lists books related to many of the articles. The books are listed under subject headings (alphabetically arranged) that are the same as the titles of the articles in the encyclopedia.

(b) General encyclopedias usually have many good maps. You find these maps in articles about the world, the continents, countries, and cities of the world, the states of the United States, and other subjects.

2. Books about your subject, or topic. Chapter 5 tells you how to find out what books a library owns and how to locate books on the shelves. But a flood of new books is published each year (in a world already full of books), and no library could possibly have them all. As you continue to do research, you will want to know whether books on certain subjects are available and, if so, what those books are.

You can find out by using reference books known by the general name *Books in Print.* There are several different volumes, clearly marked to show the years that they cover. Two of the volumes list only children's (young people's) books. Most libraries and many bookstores have these handy and well-known reference tools. The ones that you would use to find books listed by subjects are these:

> *Subject Guide to Children's Books in Print* (one volume, with lists of young people's books under more than 6,000 subjects, arranged alphabetically)

> *Subject Guide to Books in Print* (more than one volume because there are far too many listings to fit into a single volume; books are listed under subject headings, arranged alphabetically, and each volume contains listings for a certain part of the alphabet—for example, A to G, H to P, and so on; books for young people are listed along with all the others)

Other members of the *Books in Print* family list books under the names of their authors (and illustrators, too, in one case) and under their titles:

Children's Books in Print (one volume with three sections that list books under the names of their authors, their titles, and the names of their illustrators)

Books in Print: Authors (more than one volume, with a part of the alphabetical listing, under authors' names, in each volume; books for young people are included)

Books in Print: Titles (again, more than one volume; young people's books included)

3. Dictionaries and Thesauruses. As we have said in Chapter 5, a dictionary is perhaps the kind of reference book that you should choose if you could have only one kind. In choosing, you would have a wide selection. There are dictionaries for young people of different ages and grade levels, as well as dictionaries for older students and adults. In size, dictionaries may be small enough to fit into a pocket or so big and heavy that they are hard to lift. Most dictionaries have hard covers, but some are paperbacks. The largest dictionaries (called unabridged dictionaries) are the most complete—that is, they have the largest number of words.

You should take time in deciding what dictionary is best for you. Examine dictionaries in libraries and bookstores. And find out what dictionaries are available by looking under the heading "English Language—Dictionaries" in the *Subject Guide to Children's Books in Print* (or the bigger *Subject Guide*). Thesauruses are listed along with dictionaries. Perhaps a librarian would go over the list and discuss the entries with you. Librarians know quite a bit about the history of dictionaries, and they recognize the names of the best-known makers and publishers of dictionaries.

4. Atlases. Like dictionaries, atlases (collections of maps in book form) are among the most important reference tools. Chapter 5 of this book tells about atlases and the different kinds of maps that they contain. If you are thinking of buying an atlas, you will want to examine as many different kinds as possible, in your library or in bookstores. And you can look under the heading ''Atlases'' in *Books in Print* to discover all the different kinds that are available. Once you work with atlases, you begin to recognize the names of some of the best-known makers of maps, globes, and atlases, such as Hammond, National Geographic, and Rand McNally.

5. Computers. The electronics age has given us an important new research tool—the computer. Maybe you have discovered this tool and are using it to search for information in different kinds of data bases. If so, you know how exciting electronics research can be. If you have not yet had the chance, your turn may come soon. Be ready! The computer is a tool that can really turn you on to information.

Index

Abridged Readers' Guide to Periodical Literature, 39
Academic American Encyclopedia, 34
Almanacs, 38
Annual encyclopedia, 35
Antonyms, 36
Atlases, 37, 89–90
Authors
    biographical information, 84, 86
    listings in bibliographies, 74–77
    listings in *Books in Print*, 89
    listings in library catalogs, 43
    listings in *Readers' Guide to Periodical Literature*, 39–40

Back issues of periodicals, 38

Bartlett's Familiar Quotations, 38
Baseball Encyclopedia, The, 36
Bibliographies, 43, 55, 74–77
Biographies
    authors, 84, 86
    in libraries, 48
    reference books, 37
Book review cards, 80, 82
Book reviews and reports, 78–86
Books, 31, 41–48, 88–89
    listings in bibliographies, 74, 76. *See also* Reference books
Books in Print, 88–89
Books in Print: Authors, 89
Books in Print: Titles, 89

Call number of library books, 44–45

Capitalization, 70, 76
Card catalog, library, 41–45
CD-ROM's, 34
Children's Books in Print, 89
Children's Magazine Guide, 39–40
Class number of library books, 43–44
Compact disks, 34
Computers, 30–31, 72, 90
  encyclopedias, 34
  library catalogs, 42
Concise Dictionary of American Biography, 37
Concise Dictionary of American History, 36
Contents page of books, 45–46
Copyright notice in books, 33
Cover, report, 77
Crediting information sources, 55–56
Current Biography, 37, 84

Data bases, 30, 34
Dewey, Melvil, 43
Dewey Decimal System, 43–44
Diaries, 79
Dictionaries, 36, 89
  encyclopedias using "dictionary" in titles, 35
Dictionary of American Biography, 37
Dictionary of American History, 35–36

Encyclopaedia Britannica, 34
Encyclopedia Americana, 34
Encyclopedia of Sports, The, 36
Encyclopedia of World Art, 35
Encyclopedias, 34–36, 87–88
  articles about well-known people, 37, 84
  bibliographies, listing of articles in, 76

Facts, 14–15, 71–72
  in reference books, 32–33
Facts on File: A Weekly World News Digest with Cumulative Index, 41
Famous First Facts: A Record of First Happenings, Discoveries, and Inventions in American History, 38
Favorite-author file, 84, 86
Fiction, 41
  arrangement in libraries, 48
Final copy of report, 72–77
First draft of report, 66–72

Gazetteers, 37
General encyclopedias, 34–35, 87–88
Guinness Book of World Records, 38

Handwriting, 73–74

Illustrations, 29

Index cards, 52
Indexes
    books, 46–47
    encyclopedias, 35
    magazines, 39–41
    newspapers, 41
Information Age, 12–13
Information centers, 11, 30
Information Please Almanac,
    38
Information specialists, 11
Interviews, 50–51

Journals, 79
Junior Book of Authors, The,
    37, 84

Leaflets, 48
Libraries, 11, 30–31
    catalogs, 41–45
    classification systems,
        43–44, 48
    magazines and newspa-
        pers, 38
    reference section, 32
Library of Congress Classifi-
    cation, 43

Magazines, 38
    bibliographies, listing of
        articles in, 76–77
    indexes, 39–41
Maps, 37, 88–90
Margins of final copy, 74
Merit Students Encyclopedia,
    34

Microfiche, 42
Microfilm, 38
*Modern Encyclopedia of Bas-
    ketball, The*, 36
More Junior Authors, 37, 84
Museums, 49–50

National Geographic, 41
New Book of Knowledge, The,
    34, 87
*New Grove Dictionary of Mu-
    sic and Musicians*, 35
Newspapers, 38
    index, 41
New York Times Index, The,
    41
Nonfiction books, 41
    library classification sys-
        tems, 43–44, 48
Notes
    changing notes into out-
        line form, 63–64
    taking notes, 52–54

*Official Museum Directory,
    The*, 50
Opinions, 14–15, 71
    in reference books, 33
Oral book reviews, 79
Organizing ideas, 58
Outlining, 57–65

Pamphlets, 48
Paragraphs, indentation of, 74
People as sources of informa-
    tion, 50–51

Periodicals, 38
    indexes, 39–41
Physical maps, 37
Planning a report, 17
Political maps, 37
Punctuation, 70, 76

Quotations, 56

Readers' Guide to Periodical Literature, 39–40
Reading records, 79–80
Reference books, 31–41, 87–90
Relationships among subjects, 23
Reports
    definition of, 14–15
    importance of, 11–13
Researching, 30–51
Roget, Peter Mark, 36

Sentence outline, 60, 63
Sentences, 70–71
Specialized encyclopedias, 35
Spelling, 70
Statistical Abstract of the United States, 38
Subject Guide to Books in Print, 88
Subject Guide to Children's Books in Print, 88
Subject listings
    in *Books in Print*, 88
    in indexes to magazine articles, 39–40
    in library catalogs, 42

Subject of a report, 18–21
    choosing and narrowing the subject, 21–27
Synonyms, 36

Table of contents, 45
Television programs as information sources, 48–49
Thesauruses, 36, 89
Title listings
    in *Books in Print*, 89
    in library catalogs, 43
Title of a report, 26–27, 74
Title page of books, 33
Topic outline, 63

Unabridged dictionaries, 89

Vertical file, 48

Webster's New Biographical Dictionary, 37
Who's Who, 37
World Almanac and Book of Facts, 38
World Book Encyclopedia, 34, 87
World events, summaries and indexes to, 41
Writing
    book reviews and reports, 80–84
    final copy of report, 72–77
    first draft of report, 66–72

Yearbook, encyclopedia, 35

About the Author

Sue R. Brandt is a writer, a former teacher, and an editor of ency-clopedias and other books. The best part of these jobs, she says, is that they have given her a chance to work with young people and help prepare books that tell what young people want to know. Mrs. Brandt received a degree in English from the Univer-sity of Chicago. The books that she has written include *Facts About the Fifty States*, published by Franklin Watts. She thinks of Missouri as her home state, but she now lives in New York City.